The Worship Leader's Arsenal

Powerful Exhortations to Ignite Thanksgiving, Praise & Worship

Gerard Assey

The Worship Leader's Arsenal:
Powerful Exhortations to Ignite Thanksgiving, Praise & Worship

By
Gerard Assey

Published by:
Gerard Assey
19/18, Palli Arasan Street
Anna Nagar East
Chennai - 600 102

ISBN: 978-81-985691-9-6

Table of Contents

Introduction

Worship is at the very heart of God. From the beginning of creation to the end of time, worship has been the ultimate purpose of mankind—to glorify God and enjoy His presence forever. Throughout Scripture, we see that worship is not merely an act but a lifestyle, a posture of the heart, and an offering of love and adoration to our Heavenly Father. Jesus Himself declared that the Father is seeking worshippers who will worship Him in spirit and in truth (John 4:23-24). As worship leaders, we have the sacred responsibility of shepherding God's people into His presence, leading them to exalt His name with thanksgiving, praise, and worship.

The Importance of Preparation in Worship

While worship is a spiritual experience, it also requires preparation. The anointing of the Holy Spirit does not replace preparation; rather, preparation allows us to flow with the Spirit more effectively. Worship leaders must be equipped with the Word of God, for it is the foundation upon which true worship stands. When we exhort the congregation using Scripture, we are declaring the truth of who God is, stirring faith, and aligning hearts with His presence.

In 1 Corinthians 14:15, Paul says, *"I will sing with the spirit, and I will also sing with the understanding."* This means that while we engage in Spirit-led worship, we must also be intentional in our approach—bringing depth, understanding, and revelation to those we lead.

The Power of Exhortation in Worship

Exhortation plays a crucial role in worship. It is more than a mere transition between songs—it is a moment of divine invitation, a call to engage in the presence of God with faith and expectation. When we use the Word of God to exhort, we:

- ✓ **Align hearts with God's truth** – Faith comes by hearing the Word (Romans 10:17), and when we speak Scripture, we declare the unchanging nature of God.
- ✓ **Prepare the congregation spiritually** – Exhortations set the atmosphere, shifting minds from distractions to a posture of surrender and reverence.
- ✓ **Encourage engagement** – Many in the congregation may be weary or hesitant; a Spirit-led exhortation can stir their hearts to worship.
- ✓ **Magnify God above circumstances** – Worship is not dependent on emotions but on the greatness of God. Exhortations remind the people to focus on Him rather than their situations.

How to Use This Book

This book contains 52 **Thanksgiving Scriptures**, 52 **Praise Scriptures**, and 52 **Worship Scriptures**—each accompanied by a short exhortation. These are designed to help you as a worship leader flow smoothly and powerfully during your worship sets.

The structure follows a biblical pattern:

- ✓ **Thanksgiving** – We enter His presence with thanksgiving (Psalm 100:4). Use these Scriptures and exhortations to begin worship by expressing gratitude for God's goodness and faithfulness.

- ✓ **Praise** – Praise shifts the focus from our blessings to God's greatness. This is where we declare His mighty works, His power, and His glory.
- ✓ **Worship** – Worship takes us deeper into intimacy with God, surrendering fully to His presence and exalting Him in reverence and adoration.

As you lead worship, allow the Holy Spirit to guide you. Choose the scriptures and exhortations that align with the theme of your worship setlist, the leading of the Spirit, or the specific need of the congregation at that moment. These exhortations are not rigid scripts but springboards for you to personalize and expand upon as the Spirit leads.

A Call to Excellence in Worship

Worship is not a performance—it is a holy calling. As worship leaders, we are ministers before the Lord, much like the Levites who ministered in the temple. Therefore, let us approach this role with reverence, dedication, and a heart fully surrendered to Him. May this book be a tool to equip you, inspire you, and help you lead God's people into deeper encounters with His presence.

Let us worship with all that we are, for He alone is worthy! **Amen.**

Thanksgiving

52. Scriptures & Exhortations for Thanksgiving

1. 1 Thessalonians 5:16-18

"Rejoice always, pray without ceasing, give thanks in all circumstances; for this is the will of God in Christ Jesus for you."

Exhortation:

No matter the season, God calls us to thanksgiving! Today, let joy fill your heart as we lift our voices in gratitude. In every circumstance, He is faithful, and our praise declares His goodness!

---

2. Colossians 3:15-17

"Let the peace of Christ rule in your hearts, since as members of one body you were called to peace. And be thankful… Whatever you do, whether in word or deed, do it all in the name of the Lord Jesus, giving thanks to God the Father through Him."

Exhortation:

Let the peace of Christ lead you into thanksgiving! As we worship, let every word and every song be a declaration of gratitude, for He has called us into His marvelous kingdom of peace!

---

3. Philippians 4:6-7

"Do not be anxious about anything, but in every situation, by prayer and petition, with thanksgiving, present your requests to God. And the peace of God, which transcends all understanding, will guard your hearts and minds in Christ Jesus."

Exhortation:

Lay every worry at the feet of Jesus, and let thanksgiving rise in your heart! As we worship, release your burdens and receive His supernatural peace that surpasses all understanding.

---

4. 2 Corinthians 9:11
"You will be enriched in every way so that you can be generous on every occasion, and through us your generosity will result in thanksgiving to God."
Exhortation:
God blesses us so that we may be a blessing! As we give Him thanks today, let's also offer ourselves as vessels of generosity, reflecting His abundant goodness to the world.

---

5. Psalm 107:1
"Give thanks to the Lord, for He is good; His love endures forever."
Exhortation:
Our God is eternally good! His love never fades, never fails, and never ends. Let's lift up our voices in thanksgiving, declaring that He alone is worthy of all our praise!

---

6. Ephesians 5:20
"Always giving thanks to God the Father for everything, in the name of our Lord Jesus Christ."
Exhortation:
Thanksgiving is not just for moments of joy but for all things, in every season. Let's come before God with hearts full of gratitude, knowing that He is working all things for our good!

---

7. 1 Chronicles 16:34
"Give thanks to the Lord, for He is good; His love endures forever."

Exhortation:
Today, let's join in the eternal song of thanksgiving! His love has never failed and will never fail. Lift up your hands and declare the goodness of our faithful God!

---

8. Psalm 9:1
"I will give thanks to you, Lord, with all my heart; I will tell of all your wonderful deeds."
Exhortation:
Thanksgiving is not just an inward reflection—it's a declaration! As we worship, let's proclaim the mighty works of our God, testifying of His faithfulness to the world!

---

9. Psalm 28:7
"The Lord is my strength and my shield; my heart trusts in Him, and He helps me. My heart leaps for joy, and with my song I praise Him."
Exhortation:
Has the Lord been your strength? Has He been your shield? Then let your heart rejoice! With every song we sing today, let's give thanks to the One who upholds us!

---

10. Psalm 69:30
"I will praise God's name in song and glorify Him with thanksgiving."
Exhortation:
Our thanksgiving is an offering of worship! As we sing His name, let our hearts overflow with gratitude, bringing Him the honor and glory He deserves.

---

11. Psalm 118:1
"Give thanks to the Lord, for He is good; His love endures forever."

Exhortation:
God's goodness is unchanging, and His love has no end! Let's lift up our voices in thanksgiving, declaring that His mercy endures forever!

---

12. Psalm 136:1-3
"Give thanks to the Lord, for He is good. His love endures forever. Give thanks to the God of gods. His love endures forever. Give thanks to the Lord of lords: His love endures forever."
Exhortation:
Every moment of our lives is covered by His steadfast love! As we worship, let's echo heaven's song—giving thanks to the King of kings and the Lord of lords!

---

13. Daniel 6:10
"Now when Daniel learned that the decree had been published, he went home to his upstairs room where the windows opened toward Jerusalem. Three times a day he got down on his knees and prayed, giving thanks to his God, just as he had done before."
Exhortation:
True thanksgiving is not based on circumstances! Like Daniel, let's give thanks boldly, trusting that our God is in control, no matter what comes our way!

---

14. Jonah 2:9
"But I, with shouts of grateful praise, will sacrifice to You. What I have vowed I will make good. I will say, 'Salvation comes from the Lord.'"
Exhortation:
Even in the darkest places, thanksgiving has power! Let's offer up a sacrifice of praise today, declaring that our salvation comes from the Lord alone!

15. Colossians 2:6-7

"So then, just as you received Christ Jesus as Lord, continue to live your lives in Him, rooted and built up in Him, strengthened in the faith as you were taught, and overflowing with thankfulness."

Exhortation:

A heart rooted in Christ will always overflow with thanksgiving! Let's express our gratitude today as those firmly planted in His love and grace.

---

16. 1 Timothy 4:4-5

"For everything God created is good, and nothing is to be rejected if it is received with thanksgiving, because it is consecrated by the word of God and prayer."

Exhortation:

Every good gift comes from God! Let's give thanks not only for what we see but also for what He is working behind the scenes in our lives.

---

17. Hebrews 12:28

"Therefore, since we are receiving a kingdom that cannot be shaken, let us be thankful, and so worship God acceptably with reverence and awe."

Exhortation:

We are part of an unshakable kingdom! With reverence and awe, let's lift our hands in thanksgiving, worshiping the One who reigns forever!

---

18. Luke 17:15-16

"One of them, when he saw he was healed, came back, praising God in a loud voice. He threw himself at Jesus' feet and thanked Him—and he was a Samaritan."

Exhortation:

Like the one leper who returned, let's not take God's blessings for granted. Right now, let's throw ourselves at His feet in gratitude for all He has done!

---

19. Psalm 50:14

"Sacrifice thank offerings to God, fulfill your vows to the Most High."

Exhortation:

Thanksgiving is an offering that pleases the Lord! Let's bring Him our gratitude today, lifting our voices as an acceptable sacrifice of praise.

---

20. Psalm 116:17

"I will sacrifice a thank offering to You and call on the name of the Lord."

Exhortation:

When we call on His name, He answers! Let's respond with thanksgiving, offering our praise as a declaration of trust in our faithful God!

---

21. 2 Corinthians 4:15

"All this is for your benefit, so that the grace that is reaching more and more people may cause thanksgiving to overflow to the glory of God."

Exhortation:

God's grace is expanding across the earth! Let's lift our thanksgiving to Him, knowing that through us, His glory will be made known to many!

---

22. Nehemiah 12:46-47

"For long ago, in the days of David and Asaph, there had been directors for the musicians and for the songs of praise and thanksgiving to God."

Exhortation:

From generation to generation, thanksgiving has been part of worship! Today, let's take our place in this great symphony of praise to our mighty God!

---

23. Jeremiah 30:19

"From them will come songs of thanksgiving and the sound of rejoicing. I will add to their numbers, and they will not be decreased; I will bring them honor, and they will not be disdained."

Exhortation:

God is a restorer! As we sing songs of thanksgiving, let's believe that He is multiplying, blessing, and restoring every area of our lives!

---

24. 1 Chronicles 29:13

"Now, our God, we give You thanks, and praise Your glorious name."

Exhortation:

There is no name higher, no name greater than our God! Let's lift up a mighty sound of thanksgiving and praise to His glorious name today!

---

25. Psalm 95:2

"Let us come before Him with thanksgiving and extol Him with music and song."

Exhortation:

Music is a powerful expression of gratitude! As we worship, let every note and every lyric be an offering of thanksgiving to our King!

---

26. Psalm 103:1-5

"Praise the Lord, my soul; all my inmost being, praise His holy name. Praise the Lord, my soul, and forget

not all His benefits—who forgives all your sins and heals all your diseases..."

Exhortation:

God has forgiven, healed, and redeemed us! With all that is within us, let's bless His holy name and give Him the thanks He deserves!

---

27. James 1:17

"Every good and perfect gift is from above, coming down from the Father of the heavenly lights, who does not change like shifting shadows."

Exhortation:

Every blessing in our lives is a gift from our faithful Father! Let's thank Him today, knowing that He is the source of all that is good.

---

28. Psalm 92:1-2

"It is good to praise the Lord and make music to Your name, O Most High, proclaiming Your love in the morning and Your faithfulness at night."

Exhortation:

Morning or evening, God's faithfulness never fails! Let's fill this place with the sound of thanksgiving as we worship the Most High!

---

29. 2 Samuel 22:50

"Therefore I will praise You, Lord, among the nations; I will sing the praises of Your name."

Exhortation:

Our thanksgiving is a testimony to the nations! Let's lift our voices and proclaim the praises of our God, who reigns over all the earth!

---

30. Psalm 75:1

"We praise You, God, we praise You, for Your Name is near; people tell of Your wonderful deeds."

Exhortation:

God is near to us, and His works are marvelous! As we worship, let's remember all He has done and declare His goodness with thankful hearts!

---

31. Psalm 34:1

"I will bless the Lord at all times; His praise shall continually be in my mouth."

Exhortation:

Thanksgiving isn't just for the good times—it's for all times! No matter what we face, let's lift up continuous praise to our God!

---

32. 1 Chronicles 23:30

"They were also to stand every morning to thank and praise the Lord. They were to do the same in the evening."

Exhortation:

Morning and evening, let gratitude be our rhythm of worship! Let's stand together in thanksgiving, just as God's people have always done.

---

33. Acts 16:25

"About midnight Paul and Silas were praying and singing hymns to God, and the other prisoners were listening to them."

Exhortation:

Thanksgiving has power even in the darkest moments! Let's sing our praises today, knowing that worship can break every chain!

---

34. 2 Chronicles 5:13

"The trumpeters and musicians joined in unison to give praise and thanks to the Lord…They raised their voices in praise to the Lord and sang: 'He is good; His love endures forever.' Then the temple of the Lord was filled with the cloud."

Exhortation:

When we unite in thanksgiving, God's glory fills the place! Let's lift our voices in one accord and welcome His presence among us!

---

35. 2 Chronicles 20:21-22

"After consulting the people, Jehoshaphat appointed men to sing to the Lord and to praise Him for the splendor of His holiness... As they began to sing and praise, the Lord set ambushes against their enemies."

Exhortation:

Thanksgiving is a weapon! As we lift up our song of gratitude, let's trust that God is fighting our battles even now!

---

36. Ezra 3:11

"With praise and thanksgiving they sang to the Lord: 'He is good; His love toward Israel endures forever.' And all the people gave a great shout of praise to the Lord."

Exhortation:

God's love never fails! Let's join the countless generations who have declared His goodness with thanksgiving and praise!

---

37. Psalm 30:11-12

"You turned my mourning into dancing; You removed my sackcloth and clothed me with joy, that my heart may sing Your praises and not be silent."

Exhortation:

Has God turned your sorrow into joy? Let's not be silent—let's fill this place with thanksgiving for all He has done!

---

38. Isaiah 12:4-5

"Give praise to the Lord, proclaim His name; make known among the nations what He has done... Sing to the Lord, for He has done glorious things!"

Exhortation:

Thanksgiving is a testimony! Let's proclaim His name and sing of the glorious things He has done in our lives!

---

39. Deuteronomy 8:10

"When you have eaten and are satisfied, praise the Lord your God for the good land He has given you."

Exhortation:

Every blessing comes from Him! As we worship, let's remember to thank Him for His abundant provision in our lives.

---

40. 1 Corinthians 1:4-5

"I always thank my God for you because of His grace given you in Christ Jesus. For in Him you have been enriched in every way."

Exhortation:

We are enriched in Christ! Let's overflow with thanksgiving for His grace that empowers and strengthens us daily.

---

41. Philippians 1:3-5

"I thank my God every time I remember you. In all my prayers for all of you, I always pray with joy because of your partnership in the gospel."

Exhortation:

Let's give thanks for one another today! We are part of something greater—a family united in the gospel of Christ!

---

42. Psalm 119:62

"At midnight I rise to give You thanks for Your righteous laws."

Exhortation:

God's Word is worth celebrating! Even in the midnight hour, let's lift our voices in gratitude for His truth that guides us.

---

43. Psalm 145:10

"All Your works praise You, Lord; Your faithful people extol You."

Exhortation:

All creation praises Him, and so do we! Let's join the song of heaven and earth, lifting our thanksgiving to our faithful God!

---

44. Psalm 147:7

"Sing to the Lord with grateful praise; make music to our God on the harp."

Exhortation:

Our worship is a joyful sound! Let's sing with grateful hearts and make music that honors our King!

---

45. Romans 1:21

"For although they knew God, they neither glorified Him as God nor gave thanks to Him."

Exhortation:
A thankful heart keeps us close to God! Let's never forget to give Him the glory and gratitude He deserves.

---

46. Luke 2:38
"She gave thanks to God and spoke about the child to all who were looking forward to the redemption of Jerusalem."
Exhortation:
Like Anna, let's give thanks for Jesus—our Redeemer, our Savior, our King! He is worthy of all our praise!

---

47. Romans 14:6
"Whoever regards one day as special does so to the Lord. Whoever eats meat does so to the Lord, for they give thanks to God."
Exhortation:
Every part of our lives is an opportunity for thanksgiving! Let's lift up our gratitude in all we do today!

---

48. 2 Corinthians 2:14
"But thanks be to God, who always leads us as captives in Christ's triumphal procession and uses us to spread the aroma of the knowledge of Him everywhere."
Exhortation:
We walk in victory! As we give thanks, let's declare that we are led by Christ in triumph!

---

49. Colossians 4:2
"Devote yourselves to prayer, being watchful and thankful."

Exhortation:
Thanksgiving is an essential part of prayer! Let's take a moment to thank God for His faithfulness in our lives.

---

50. Revelation 7:12
"'Amen! Praise and glory and wisdom and thanks and honor and power and strength be to our God forever and ever. Amen!'"
Exhortation:
This is heaven's song! Let's lift our voices in agreement, giving all thanks and honor to our God forever!

---

51. Psalm 140:13
"Surely the righteous will praise Your name, and the upright will live in Your presence."
Exhortation:
His presence is our dwelling place! Let's come before Him with thankful hearts, knowing He is always with us.

---

52. Psalm 138:1-2
"I will praise You, Lord, with all my heart... I will bow down toward Your holy temple and will praise Your name for Your unfailing love and Your faithfulness."
Exhortation:
With all our hearts, let's worship Him! His love never fails, and His faithfulness endures forever!

Praise

52. Scriptures & Exhortations for Praise

1. Psalm 150:1-6
"Praise the Lord. Praise God in His sanctuary; praise Him in His mighty heavens... Let everything that has breath praise the Lord!"
Exhortation:
If you have breath in your lungs, you have a reason to praise! Let's lift our voices and exalt the Lord with everything within us!

---

2. Psalm 148:1-14
"Praise the Lord from the heavens; praise Him in the heights above... Let them praise the name of the Lord, for His name alone is exalted."
Exhortation:
The heavens declare His glory, and so should we! Let's join the song of creation and magnify the name of the Lord!

---

3. Psalm 149:1-5
"Sing to the Lord a new song, His praise in the assembly of His faithful people... Let His faithful people rejoice in this honor and sing for joy on their beds."
Exhortation:
We are His faithful ones! Let's sing a new song of praise and rejoice in the honor of worshiping our great King!

---

4. Psalm 147:1
"Praise the Lord. How good it is to sing praises to our God, how pleasant and fitting to praise Him!"

Exhortation:
There's nothing more beautiful than praising our God! Let's lift our voices together in joyful worship!

---

5. Isaiah 25:1
"Lord, You are my God; I will exalt You and praise Your name, for in perfect faithfulness You have done wonderful things."
Exhortation:
Has God done wonderful things for you? Let's exalt His name and declare His faithfulness in our praise today!

---

6. Exodus 15:1-2
"I will sing to the Lord, for He is highly exalted... The Lord is my strength and my defense; He has become my salvation."
Exhortation:
God is our strength and salvation! Just as Israel sang in victory, let's lift up a mighty song of praise to our Deliverer!

---

7. Psalm 33:1-3
"Sing joyfully to the Lord, you righteous; it is fitting for the upright to praise Him... Sing to Him a new song; play skillfully, and shout for joy!"
Exhortation:
It's fitting for us to praise Him! Let's sing with joy and lift up a shout of victory to our King!

---

8. Psalm 135:1-3
"Praise the Lord. Praise the name of the Lord; praise Him, you servants of the Lord... Praise the Lord, for the Lord is good."

Exhortation:
We, His servants, are called to praise! Let's declare His goodness with hearts full of gratitude!

---

9. Psalm 96:1-4
"Sing to the Lord a new song; sing to the Lord, all the earth... For great is the Lord and most worthy of praise."
Exhortation:
Let's sing a new song today, declaring that our God is great and worthy of all our praise!

---

10. Psalm 98:4-6
"Shout for joy to the Lord, all the earth, burst into jubilant song with music... Make music to the Lord with the harp, with the sound of singing!"
Exhortation:
Let's not hold back—let's burst into joyful praise and fill this place with the sound of worship!

---

11. Psalm 89:1
"I will sing of the Lord's great love forever; with my mouth I will make Your faithfulness known through all generations."
Exhortation:
God's love never fails! Let's lift our voices and proclaim His faithfulness to all generations!

---

12. Hebrews 2:12
"I will declare Your name to my brothers and sisters; in the assembly, I will sing Your praises."
Exhortation:
We are here to declare His name! Let's sing with boldness and magnify the Lord together!

---

13. Luke 19:37-40

"The whole crowd of disciples began joyfully to praise God in loud voices... 'If they keep quiet, the stones will cry out.'"

Exhortation:

Don't let the rocks take your place! Let's raise a loud praise that echoes through heaven and earth!

---

14. Matthew 21:9

"The crowds shouted, 'Hosanna to the Son of David! Blessed is He who comes in the name of the Lord!'"

Exhortation:

Just as they welcomed Jesus with shouts of praise, let's lift up our own "Hosanna" to our King today!

---

15. 1 Peter 2:9

"You are a chosen people... that you may declare the praises of Him who called you out of darkness into His wonderful light."

Exhortation:

We've been brought out of darkness! Let's declare His praises and shine His light through our worship!

---

16. 1 Chronicles 16:25-29

"For great is the Lord and most worthy of praise... Worship the Lord in the splendor of His holiness."

Exhortation:

Our God is great and worthy of our highest praise! Let's worship Him in the beauty of His holiness!

---

17. Psalm 103:20-22

"Praise the Lord, you His angels... Praise the Lord, all His works everywhere in His dominion."

Exhortation:
All of creation praises Him! Let's join heaven's song and give Him the glory He deserves!

---

18. Psalm 63:3-5
"Because Your love is better than life, my lips will glorify You. I will praise You as long as I live."
Exhortation:
His love is greater than life itself! Let's glorify Him with all that we are!

---

19. Psalm 42:11
"Put your hope in God, for I will yet praise Him, my Savior and my God."
Exhortation:
Even in difficult times, we praise! Let's put our hope in Him and declare His goodness!

---

20. Psalm 34:2-3
"I will glory in the Lord; let the afflicted hear and rejoice. Glorify the Lord with me; let us exalt His name together!"
Exhortation:
We are called to exalt Him together! Let's lift our voices as one and glorify our King!

---

21. Psalm 71:8
"My mouth is filled with Your praise, declaring Your splendor all day long."
Exhortation:
May our worship not be just for today—let's be filled with His praise at all times!

---

22. Psalm 106:1-2

"Praise the Lord. Give thanks to the Lord, for He is good; His love endures forever."

Exhortation:

His love is everlasting! Let's give thanks and lift up our highest praise!

---

23. Isaiah 12:5

"Sing to the Lord, for He has done glorious things; let this be known to all the world."

Exhortation:

Let's sing of His glorious deeds and make His name known everywhere we go!

---

24. Psalm 113:1-3

"Praise the Lord. Let the name of the Lord be praised, both now and forevermore."

Exhortation:

His praise is eternal! Let's lift His name now and forever!

---

25. Psalm 8:1-2

"Lord, our Lord, how majestic is Your name in all the earth!"

Exhortation:

His name is majestic! Let's give Him the honor and praise that belongs to Him alone!

---

26. Psalm 29:1-2

"Ascribe to the Lord, you heavenly beings, ascribe to the Lord glory and strength. Ascribe to the Lord the glory due His name; worship the Lord in the splendor of His holiness."

Exhortation:

Let's give the Lord the glory due His name! He alone is worthy of our highest praise!

---

27. Psalm 68:4

"Sing to God, sing in praise of His name, extol Him who rides on the clouds; rejoice before Him—His name is the Lord."

Exhortation:

Our God reigns! Let's lift our voices in joyful praise to His mighty name!

---

28. Psalm 86:12

"I will praise You, Lord my God, with all my heart; I will glorify Your name forever."

Exhortation:

Let's praise Him with all our hearts today and forevermore!

---

29. Psalm 108:3-4

"I will praise You, Lord, among the nations; I will sing of You among the peoples. For great is Your love, higher than the heavens."

Exhortation:

God's love reaches higher than the heavens! Let's declare His greatness among all nations!

---

30. Revelation 5:12-13

"Worthy is the Lamb, who was slain, to receive power and wealth and wisdom and strength and honor and glory and praise!"

Exhortation:

Jesus is worthy of all honor, glory, and praise! Let's worship the Lamb of God!

---

31. Psalm 9:11

"Sing the praises of the Lord, enthroned in Zion; proclaim among the nations what He has done."

Exhortation:

Let's make His name known! Sing His praises and proclaim His goodness to all the world!

---

32. Psalm 22:22

"I will declare Your name to my people; in the assembly, I will praise You."

Exhortation:

In the presence of God's people, let's lift high the name of the Lord!

---

33. Deuteronomy 10:21

"He is the one you praise; He is your God, who performed for you those great and awesome wonders you saw with your own eyes."

Exhortation:

Has God done great things in your life? Let's lift up a shout of praise for His mighty works!

---

34. Isaiah 43:21

"The people I formed for Myself, that they may proclaim My praise."

Exhortation:

We were created to praise Him! Let's do what we were made for and glorify His name!

---

35. Psalm 145:1-3

"I will exalt You, my God the King; I will praise Your name for ever and ever... Great is the Lord and most worthy of praise!"

Exhortation:
God is great and greatly to be praised! Let's exalt His name forever!

---

36. Psalm 92:1-4
"It is good to praise the Lord and make music to Your name, O Most High."
Exhortation:
There is joy in praising our God! Let's sing and rejoice in His goodness!

---

37. Romans 15:11
"Praise the Lord, all you Gentiles; let all the peoples extol Him."
Exhortation:
Praise is for everyone! Let's join together, every tribe and nation, in lifting up His name!

---

38. 2 Samuel 22:4
"I called to the Lord, who is worthy of praise, and have been saved from my enemies."
Exhortation:
Our God is a mighty deliverer! Let's call on His name and give Him the praise He deserves!

---

39. 2 Chronicles 20:22
"As they began to sing and praise, the Lord set ambushes against their enemies."
Exhortation:
Praise is powerful! As we worship, let's trust God to fight our battles for us!

---

40. Isaiah 61:3
"To bestow on them a garment of praise instead of a spirit of despair."

Exhortation:
If you feel heavy today, put on the garment of praise! Let's trade despair for joy in the Lord!

---

41. Psalm 105:2
"Sing to Him, sing praise to Him; tell of all His wonderful acts."
Exhortation:
Let's sing of His wonders and declare His greatness to all!

---

42. Psalm 66:8
"Praise our God, all peoples, let the sound of His praise be heard!"
Exhortation:
Don't keep your praise silent—let's lift up a mighty sound to our King!

---

43. Psalm 111:1
"Praise the Lord. I will extol the Lord with all my heart in the council of the upright and in the assembly."
Exhortation:
With all our hearts, let's give God the highest praise together!

---

44. Acts 2:46-47
"They broke bread in their homes and ate together with glad and sincere hearts, praising God and enjoying the favor of all the people."
Exhortation:
Let's come together in unity, praising God with joyful hearts!

---

45. Revelation 19:5
"Then a voice came from the throne, saying: 'Praise our God, all you His servants, you who fear Him, both great and small!'"
Exhortation:
A command from heaven itself—let's lift our voices and praise the Lord!

---

46. Psalm 66:1-2
"Shout for joy to God, all the earth! Sing the glory of His name; make His praise glorious."
Exhortation:
Let's not hold back—make His praise glorious with shouts of joy!

---

47. Psalm 98:1
"Sing to the Lord a new song, for He has done marvelous things."
Exhortation:
Our God does marvelous things! Let's sing a fresh song of praise to Him!

---

48. Psalm 40:3
"He put a new song in my mouth, a hymn of praise to our God."
Exhortation:
If God has given you a new song, sing it out in worship to Him!

---

49. Job 1:21
"The Lord gave and the Lord has taken away; blessed be the name of the Lord."
Exhortation:
Even in trials, we bless His name. Let's praise Him in every season!

50. Psalm 81:1-2

"Sing for joy to God our strength; shout aloud to the God of Jacob!"

Exhortation:

He is our strength—let's sing and shout for joy in His presence!

51. Philippians 2:9-11

"God exalted Him to the highest place and gave Him the name that is above every name... that every tongue acknowledge that Jesus Christ is Lord."

Exhortation:

His name is above every name! Let's declare that Jesus Christ is Lord!

52. Psalm 145:21

"My mouth will speak in praise of the Lord. Let every creature praise His holy name forever and ever."

Exhortation:

Let every creature, every voice, every heart lift up praise to our King forever!

Worship

52. Scriptures & Exhortations for Worship

1. John 4:23-24
"Yet a time is coming and has now come when the true worshipers will worship the Father in the Spirit and in truth, for they are the kind of worshipers the Father seeks. God is Spirit, and His worshipers must worship in the Spirit and in truth."
Exhortation:
God is looking for true worshipers! Let's surrender our hearts and worship Him in Spirit and in truth!

---

2. Matthew 4:10
"Jesus said to him, 'Away from me, Satan! For it is written: Worship the Lord your God, and serve Him only.'"
Exhortation:
Our worship belongs to God alone! Let's lift Him high and declare that He alone is worthy!

---

3. Psalm 99:5
"Exalt the Lord our God and worship at His footstool; He is holy."
Exhortation:
Let's bow before His presence and worship our holy and mighty God!

---

4. Psalm 29:2
"Ascribe to the Lord the glory due His name; worship the Lord in the splendor of His holiness."
Exhortation:
Let's give God the glory He deserves and worship Him in the beauty of holiness!

---

5. 1 Samuel 15:22

"Does the Lord delight in burnt offerings and sacrifices as much as in obeying the Lord? To obey is better than sacrifice."

Exhortation:

Worship isn't just a song—it's a life of obedience! Let's honor Him with our hearts and actions!

---

6. Revelation 15:4

"Who will not fear You, Lord, and bring glory to Your name? For You alone are holy. All nations will come and worship before You."

Exhortation:

One day, every nation will bow before Him. Let's begin now and worship our holy God!

---

7. Nehemiah 9:6

"You alone are the Lord. You made the heavens, even the highest heavens, and all their starry host... and the multitudes of heaven worship You."

Exhortation:

The heavens declare His glory! Let's join the multitudes and worship our Creator!

---

8. Exodus 34:14

"Do not worship any other god, for the Lord, whose name is Jealous, is a jealous God."

Exhortation:

Our worship belongs to God alone—let's give Him our whole heart!

---

9. Deuteronomy 10:21

"He is the one you praise; He is your God, who performed for you those great and awesome wonders you saw with your own eyes."

Exhortation:

Has God done great things in your life? Let's worship Him with awe and gratitude!

---

10. Philippians 3:3

"For it is we who are the circumcision, we who serve God by His Spirit, who boast in Christ Jesus, and who put no confidence in the flesh."

Exhortation:

True worship comes from the Spirit! Let's boast in Christ alone and worship Him with all we are!

---

11. Psalm 86:9-10

"All the nations You have made will come and worship before You, Lord; they will bring glory to Your name. For You are great and do marvelous deeds; You alone are God."

Exhortation:

He alone is God! Let's bring Him glory as we worship His greatness!

---

12. Psalm 95:6

"Come, let us bow down in worship, let us kneel before the Lord our Maker."

Exhortation:

Let's humble ourselves before our Maker and worship Him with reverence!

---

13. Psalm 100:2

"Worship the Lord with gladness; come before Him with joyful songs."

Exhortation:
Worship is a joy! Let's enter His presence with singing and gladness!

---

14. Revelation 22:9
"But he said to me, 'Do not do that! I am a fellow servant with you and with your fellow prophets and with all who keep the words of this scroll. Worship God!'"
Exhortation:
All worship belongs to God alone! Let's fix our eyes on Him and worship Him alone!

---

15. Isaiah 66:23
"From one New Moon to another and from one Sabbath to another, all mankind will come and bow down before Me," says the Lord.
Exhortation:
One day, all mankind will worship Him—let's start now, bowing before our King!

---

16. 2 Kings 17:36
"But the Lord, who brought you up out of Egypt with mighty power and outstretched arm, is the one you must worship."
Exhortation:
He is our Deliverer! Let's worship Him for His mighty power and faithfulness!

---

17. Luke 4:8
"Jesus answered, 'It is written: Worship the Lord your God and serve Him only.'"
Exhortation:
Jesus set the example—our worship belongs to God alone! Let's lift Him high!

18. Romans 14:11

"It is written: 'As surely as I live,' says the Lord, 'every knee will bow before Me; every tongue will acknowledge God.'"

Exhortation:

One day, every knee will bow. Let's choose to bow before Him now in worship!

---

19. Psalm 96:9

"Worship the Lord in the splendor of His holiness; tremble before Him, all the earth."

Exhortation:

Let's stand in awe of His holiness and worship Him with reverence and honor!

---

20. Isaiah 6:3

"And they were calling to one another: 'Holy, holy, holy is the Lord Almighty; the whole earth is full of His glory.'"

Exhortation:

He is holy! Let's join the angels in declaring His holiness in worship!

---

21. Revelation 14:7

"He said in a loud voice, 'Fear God and give Him glory, because the hour of His judgment has come. Worship Him who made the heavens, the earth, the sea and the springs of water.'"

Exhortation:

Our God is the Creator of all! Let's worship Him with awe and reverence!

---

22. Psalm 132:7

"Let us go to His dwelling place, let us worship at His footstool."

Exhortation:

Let's enter His presence with reverence and worship at His feet!

---

23. 1 Corinthians 14:25

"So they will fall down and worship God, exclaiming, 'God is really among you!'"

Exhortation:

When we worship, His presence fills the place! Let's surrender and acknowledge that He is here!

---

24. Exodus 20:3-5

"You shall have no other gods before Me... You shall not bow down to them or worship them; for I, the Lord your God, am a jealous God."

Exhortation:

Let's cast aside every idol and worship God alone with undivided hearts!

---

25. Psalm 145:5

"They speak of the glorious splendor of Your majesty—and I will meditate on Your wonderful works."

Exhortation:

Let's meditate on His majesty and worship Him for His glorious splendor!

---

26. Isaiah 29:13

"The Lord says: 'These people come near to me with their mouth and honor me with their lips, but their hearts are far from me. Their worship of me is based on merely human rules they have been taught.'"

Exhortation:
True worship is from the heart! Let's not just sing the words—let's give Him our whole hearts in worship!

---

27. Psalm 97:7
"All who worship images are put to shame, those who boast in idols—worship Him, all you gods!"
Exhortation:
Let's cast down every idol and worship the one true God who reigns forever!

---

28. 1 Chronicles 16:29
"Ascribe to the Lord the glory due His name; bring an offering and come before Him. Worship the Lord in the splendor of His holiness."
Exhortation:
Our worship is an offering! Let's give Him the glory due His name with all that we are!

---

29. 1 Kings 8:60-61
"So that all the peoples of the earth may know that the Lord is God and that there is no other. And may your hearts be fully committed to the Lord our God, to live by His decrees and obey His commands, as at this time."
Exhortation:
Let's worship with fully committed hearts, declaring to the world that our God alone is Lord!

---

30. Romans 12:1
"Therefore, I urge you, brothers and sisters, in view of God's mercy, to offer your bodies as a living sacrifice, holy and pleasing to God—this is your true and proper worship."

Exhortation:
Worship is more than a song—it's a life laid down in surrender! Let's offer ourselves as living sacrifices!

---

31. Revelation 5:14
"The four living creatures said, 'Amen,' and the elders fell down and worshiped."
Exhortation:
All of heaven bows before Him! Let's join the heavenly hosts in worship!

---

32. Genesis 22:5
"He said to his servants, 'Stay here with the donkey while I and the boy go over there. We will worship and then we will come back to you.'"
Exhortation:
Worship requires faith and obedience! Let's trust Him as we worship with surrendered hearts!

---

33. Revelation 11:16
"And the twenty-four elders, who were seated on their thrones before God, fell on their faces and worshiped God."
Exhortation:
Let's humble ourselves in His presence and worship Him with awe and reverence!

---

34. Psalm 5:7
"But I, by Your great love, can come into Your house; in reverence I bow down toward Your holy temple."
Exhortation:
We enter His presence by His grace! Let's bow before Him with reverence and love!

---

35. Exodus 23:25

"Worship the Lord your God, and His blessing will be on your food and water. I will take away sickness from among you."

Exhortation:

There is blessing in worship! Let's worship Him with faith, knowing He is our provider and healer!

---

36. Psalm 71:22-23

"I will praise You with the harp for Your faithfulness, my God; I will sing praise to You with the lyre, Holy One of Israel. My lips will shout for joy when I sing praise to You—I whom You have delivered."

Exhortation:

If He has delivered you, let your lips shout for joy in worship!

---

37. Psalm 84:1-2

"How lovely is Your dwelling place, Lord Almighty! My soul yearns, even faints, for the courts of the Lord; my heart and my flesh cry out for the living God."

Exhortation:

Our hearts long for Him! Let's worship with a deep hunger for His presence!

---

38. Psalm 138:2

"I will bow down toward Your holy temple and will praise Your name for Your unfailing love and Your faithfulness."

Exhortation:

His love never fails! Let's bow before Him and worship in gratitude!

---

39. Hebrews 1:6

"And again, when God brings His firstborn into the world, He says, 'Let all God's angels worship Him.'"

Exhortation:

Even the angels worship Him—let's lift our voices and join them in praise!

---

40. Psalm 146:1-2

"Praise the Lord. I will praise the Lord all my life; I will sing praise to my God as long as I live."

Exhortation:

Worship is for a lifetime! Let's praise Him every day of our lives!

---

41. Psalm 35:18

"I will give You thanks in the great assembly; among the throngs I will praise You."

Exhortation:

Let's lift our voices together and worship Him in unity!

---

42. Zephaniah 3:17

"The Lord your God is with you, the Mighty Warrior who saves. He will take great delight in you; in His love He will no longer rebuke you, but will rejoice over you with singing."

Exhortation:

God rejoices over us with singing! Let's respond with worship and adoration!

---

43. Revelation 19:10

"At this I fell at his feet to worship him. But he said to me, 'Don't do that! I am a fellow servant with you and with your brothers and sisters who hold to the testimony of Jesus. Worship God!'"

Exhortation:
Worship belongs to God alone! Let's fix our eyes on Jesus and give Him all the glory!

---

44. Psalm 68:26
"Praise God in the great congregation; praise the Lord in the assembly of Israel."
Exhortation:
Let's lift up our voices together and praise the Lord in the congregation!

---

45. Isaiah 12:6
"Shout aloud and sing for joy, people of Zion, for great is the Holy One of Israel among you."
Exhortation:
Let's shout for joy—our God is great and worthy of praise!

---

46. Exodus 15:11
"Who among the gods is like You, Lord? Who is like You—majestic in holiness, awesome in glory, working wonders?"
Exhortation:
There is none like Him! Let's worship His majesty and glory!

---

47. Hebrews 10:19-22
"Let us draw near to God with a sincere heart and with the full assurance that faith brings."
Exhortation:
Through Christ, we can boldly enter His presence! Let's worship Him with faith!

---

48. Malachi 1:11

"My name will be great among the nations, from where the sun rises to where it sets. In every place incense and pure offerings will be brought to me, because my name will be great among the nations."

Exhortation:

All nations will worship Him! Let's exalt His name across the earth!

---

49. Daniel 3:28

"Then Nebuchadnezzar said, 'Praise be to the God of Shadrach, Meshach, and Abednego, who has sent His angel and rescued His servants!'"

Exhortation:

God delivers those who trust in Him! Let's worship the God who saves!

---

50. Deuteronomy 8:19

"If you ever forget the Lord your God and follow other gods… you will surely be destroyed."

Exhortation:

Let's never forget our God! Let's worship Him with undivided hearts!

---

51. 2 Chronicles 29:28

"The whole assembly bowed in worship, while the musicians played and the trumpets sounded."

Exhortation:

Let's join in with music and voices lifted high in worship!

---

52. Psalm 22:27

"All the ends of the earth will remember and turn to the Lord, and all the families of the nations will bow down before Him."

Exhortation:

Every nation will bow! Let's worship Him now and forever!

Exclusively on Worship (Longer Exhortations)

1. 1 Chronicles 16:10-12

"Glory in his holy name; let the hearts of those who seek the LORD rejoice! Seek the LORD and his strength; seek his presence continually! Remember the wondrous works that he has done, his miracles and the judgments he uttered,"

Exhortation: Worship is a response to the greatness of our God! Rejoice in Him, for His name is holy and worthy of all honor. Seek Him not just in times of need but continually, for He is your source of strength. Remember the mighty works He has done in your life—the miracles, the deliverances, the answered prayers. Let gratitude and praise rise in your heart, for the God who was faithful yesterday is the same today and forever!

---

2. Isaiah 40:28-29

"Have you not known? Have you not heard? The LORD is the everlasting God, the Creator of the ends of the earth. He does not faint or grow weary; his understanding is unsearchable. He gives power to the faint, and to him who has no might he increases strength."

Exhortation: Worship the Lord, the Everlasting God, who never tires or grows weary! His strength is inexhaustible, and His wisdom is beyond measure. When you feel weak, know that He is your source of power. Lift your voice in praise, knowing that He upholds you and strengthens you for the journey ahead. He is the Creator of all things, yet He cares intimately for you—so come before Him in awe and worship!

---

3. Psalm 95:1-7

"Oh come, let us sing to the Lord; let us make a joyful noise to the rock of our salvation! Let us come into his presence with thanksgiving; let us make a joyful noise to him with songs of praise! For the Lord is a great God, and a great King above all gods..."

Exhortation: Worship is not just a quiet reflection—it is an overflow of joy and gratitude! Come before the Lord with a song in your heart, for He is the Rock of your salvation. He is the King above all kings, and in His hands, He holds the entire universe. Let your worship be filled with thanksgiving and reverence, for you are His sheep, and He is your Good Shepherd. Bow before Him, for He is worthy of all honor and praise!

---

4. Revelation 4:11

"Worthy are you, our Lord and God, to receive glory and honor and power, for you created all things, and by your will they existed and were created."

Exhortation: Worship the Lord, for He is worthy of all glory, honor, and power! Everything that exists—every star, every mountain, every life—was created by Him and for Him. He is sovereign over all creation, and yet He invites us into His presence. Lift up your heart in worship, for there is no one like our God. Let every breath you take be an offering of praise to the One who holds all things together!

---

5. Hebrews 13:15

"Through him then let us continually offer up a sacrifice of praise to God, that is, the fruit of lips that acknowledge his name."

Exhortation: Worship is not just for when things are going well—it is a continual offering to God! Even in difficult times, let your lips declare His goodness. Praise Him not because of circumstances, but because He is always worthy. Your worship is a sweet fragrance before the throne of God. Let your life be filled with gratitude, acknowledging His name in all you do!

---

6. Psalm 100:4

"Enter his gates with thanksgiving, and his courts with praise! Give thanks to him; bless his name!"

Exhortation: The key to entering God's presence is thanksgiving! Before you ask Him for anything, thank Him for all He has already done. Worship Him with a heart full of gratitude, for He is good and His love endures forever. Bless His name with songs of praise, and let your life be a testimony of His faithfulness. Approach Him with joy, for He delights in the praises of His people!

---

7. Daniel 2:19-23

"Blessed be the name of God forever and ever, to whom belong wisdom and might. He changes times and seasons; he removes kings and sets up kings..."

Exhortation: Worship the God of wisdom and power! He alone controls the times and seasons of your life. There is nothing hidden from Him—He sees what is in the darkness and brings revelation to those who seek Him. Give thanks for His sovereignty, for He is the One who lifts up and brings down. Worship

Him with confidence, knowing that your life is in His hands!

---

8. Romans 12:1
"I appeal to you therefore, brothers, by the mercies of God, to present your bodies as a living sacrifice, holy and acceptable to God, which is your spiritual worship."
Exhortation: Worship is not just about songs—it is about a surrendered life! Offer yourself completely to God, for true worship is living in obedience to Him. Let every thought, word, and action reflect your devotion to the Lord. He has given you His mercy, so respond with a heart fully devoted to Him. Worship Him not just with your lips, but with your life!

---

9. Psalm 59:16-17
"But I will sing of your strength; I will sing aloud of your steadfast love in the morning..."
Exhortation: Worship the Lord for His unfailing love and strength! No matter what challenges you face, He is your fortress and refuge. Begin each day with a song of praise, declaring His faithfulness over your life. The enemy may come against you, but the Lord is your shield. Worship Him boldly, for He never fails His people!

---

10. Psalm 29:2
"Ascribe to the LORD the glory due his name; worship the LORD in the splendor of holiness."
Exhortation: Give God the honor He deserves! Worship is not just about what He has done for you—it is about who He is. Approach Him in reverence, for He is clothed in majesty and holiness. Let your

worship be pure, set apart for Him alone. Exalt His name, for He reigns in beauty and splendor!

---

11. Revelation 5:9
"Worthy are you to take the scroll and to open its seals, for you were slain, and by your blood you ransomed people for God from every tribe and language and people and nation…"
Exhortation: Worship the Lamb who was slain! Jesus paid the ultimate price to redeem us, and now He reigns in victory. Let your praise rise with the multitudes in heaven, declaring His worthiness. Every nation and tribe will one day bow before Him—so begin now, worshiping the King who gave His life for you!

---

12. Psalm 96:1-3
"Oh sing to the Lord a new song; sing to the Lord, all the earth! Sing to the Lord, bless his name; tell of his salvation from day to day. Declare his glory among the nations, his marvelous works among all the peoples!"
Exhortation: Worship is not just for a moment—it is a lifestyle! Sing a new song to the Lord, for His mercies are new every morning. Let all the earth lift up His name in praise, for He alone is worthy! Speak of His salvation daily—testify of His goodness and proclaim His glory to the nations. Let your worship be a light that draws others to know the greatness of our God!

---

13. John 4:23-24
"But the hour is coming, and is now here, when the true worshipers will worship the Father in spirit and truth, for the Father is seeking such people to

worship him. God is spirit, and those who worship him must worship in spirit and truth."

Exhortation: Worship is not about a place, a ritual, or a performance—it is about the heart! True worshipers worship in spirit and in truth, aligning their hearts with God's will. He seeks those who come to Him with sincerity, not just with empty words. Let your worship be filled with truth—knowing who He is and honoring Him with your whole being. Seek Him with all your heart, and He will draw near to you!

---

14. Psalm 150:1-6

"Praise the Lord! Praise God in his sanctuary; praise him in his mighty heavens! Praise him for his mighty deeds; praise him according to his excellent greatness!"

Exhortation: Worship God with everything you have! Praise Him in the sanctuary, in your home, in your workplace—wherever you are! Celebrate His mighty deeds, for He has done great things. Use every instrument, every voice, every talent to bring Him glory. Let everything that has breath praise the Lord! Worship is not just for Sunday—it is for every moment of your life!

---

15. 2 Chronicles 5:13-14

"And it was the duty of the trumpeters and singers to make themselves heard in unison in praise and thanksgiving to the Lord… the glory of the Lord filled the house of God."

Exhortation: There is power in unified worship! When God's people lift their voices together in praise and thanksgiving, His presence fills the place. Worship prepares the atmosphere for God's glory to manifest. As you worship, expect His presence to surround you, to fill your home, your church, and your life. He dwells in the praises of His people—so lift your voice and glorify His name!

---

16. Acts 16:25-26

"About midnight Paul and Silas were praying and singing hymns to God, and the prisoners were listening to them, and suddenly there was a great earthquake, so that the foundations of the prison were shaken."

Exhortation: Worship has the power to break chains! Even in the darkest night, when all seems lost, lift up a song of praise. Paul and Silas worshiped in their prison, and God responded with deliverance. Your worship can shake the foundations of your situation, opening doors and setting captives free. Let your praise rise even in trials, for your breakthrough is on the way!

---

17. Matthew 4:10

"Then Jesus said to him, 'Be gone, Satan! For it is written, You shall worship the Lord your God and him only shall you serve.'"

Exhortation: Worship is a weapon against the enemy! When the devil tempted Jesus, He responded with the Word, declaring that worship belongs to God alone. Worship keeps your heart aligned with the Lord and silences every lie of the enemy. Let your devotion be undivided—serve and worship the Lord with all your heart, and the enemy will flee!

---

18. Psalm 34:1

"I will bless the Lord at all times; his praise shall continually be in my mouth."

Exhortation: Worship is not seasonal—it is constant! Bless the Lord at all times, in every situation, whether in joy or sorrow. Let praise be the language of your heart, overflowing in every word you speak. When you choose to worship in all circumstances, you declare your trust in God's sovereignty. Let praise be your lifestyle, for He is always worthy!

---

19. Nehemiah 9:6

"You are the Lord, you alone. You have made heaven, the heaven of heavens, with all their host, the earth and all that is on it, the seas and all that is in them; and you preserve all of them; and the host of heaven worships you."

Exhortation: Worship the Creator of all things! The heavens declare His glory, and the angels worship Him continually. He sustains all life—every star, every ocean, every creature depends on Him. If all creation praises Him, how much more should we, His redeemed people? Lift up your worship to the One who alone is God, the Maker and Sustainer of all things!

---

20. Habakkuk 3:17-18

"Though the fig tree should not blossom, nor fruit be on the vines… yet I will rejoice in the Lord; I will take joy in the God of my salvation."

Exhortation: Worship is not dependent on circumstances—it is a choice! Even when things seem barren, when prayers seem unanswered, choose to rejoice in the Lord. He is your salvation, your strength, your joy! Worship through the trials, for your faith declares that God is still in control. No matter what, He is worthy of your praise!

---

21. Exodus 15:1-2

"Then Moses and the people of Israel sang this song to the Lord, saying, 'I will sing to the Lord, for he has triumphed gloriously; the horse and his rider he has thrown into the sea. The Lord is my strength and my song, and he has become my salvation.'"

Exhortation: Worship is a response to God's victory! When the Israelites crossed the Red Sea and saw their enemies defeated, they lifted up a song of praise. Has God delivered you? Has He saved you? Sing to Him! He is your strength, your song, and your salvation. Worship Him with all your heart, for He has triumphed gloriously in your life!

---

22. Philippians 2:9-11

"Therefore God has highly exalted him and bestowed on him the name that is above every name, so that at the name of Jesus every knee should bow, in heaven and on earth and under the earth, and every tongue confess that Jesus Christ is Lord, to the glory of God the Father."

Exhortation: Worship the name above all names—Jesus Christ! One day, every knee will bow before Him, and every tongue will declare His Lordship. But we don't have to wait until that day—we can worship Him now! Honor Him with your life, your words, and your heart. Proclaim His name boldly, for He is worthy of all glory!

---

23. Psalm 146:1-2

"Praise the Lord! Praise the Lord, O my soul! I will praise the Lord as long as I live; I will sing praises to my God while I have my being."

Exhortation: Worship is for a lifetime! As long as you have breath, let your soul praise the Lord. Make worship your daily habit, not just on special occasions. Let your life be a melody of praise to your God. He is faithful, He is good, and He is worthy of your worship every single day!

Final Encouragement:
Worship is not just about singing—it is about a heart fully surrendered to God. It is about recognizing who He is and responding with awe, gratitude, and devotion. Whether in joy or trials, let your worship be an offering that rises before His throne. For He alone is worthy, forever and ever!

Now, go forth and worship!

Conclusion

Worship is more than just singing songs—it is a divine invitation to encounter the presence of God. As worship leaders, we have the privilege and responsibility of guiding God's people into His courts with thanksgiving, praise, and worship. Through this journey, the Word of God must remain our foundation, as it fuels our exhortations, strengthens faith, and shifts the atmosphere.

This book has provided a collection of **Thanksgiving, Praise, and Worship Scriptures**, each paired with a short exhortation to equip and inspire you in leading worship. However, beyond using these pre-prepared exhortations, it is essential to learn how to develop your own, allowing the Holy Spirit to breathe fresh revelation into your words.

How to Develop Exhortations Using the Word of God

Crafting an exhortation involves more than just reading a scripture aloud—it is about rightly dividing the Word, making it personal, and delivering it in a way that stirs the hearts of the congregation. Below is a step-by-step method to develop powerful, Spirit-filled exhortations:

Step 1: Choose a Relevant Scripture

Seek the Holy Spirit's guidance on what the congregation needs at that moment.

Consider the theme of the worship setlist—is it focused on victory, surrender, adoration, or gratitude?

Select a verse that aligns with the spiritual atmosphere or season the church is in.

Step 2: Understand the Context of the Scripture

Read the surrounding verses to understand the historical and spiritual background.

Ask: Who was speaking? Who was being addressed? What was the situation?

Cross-reference with other supporting scriptures to gain a fuller understanding.

Step 3: Identify the Core Message for Worship

Break the verse down into its **main themes** (e.g., thanksgiving, God's power, faithfulness, holiness).

Focus on how the scripture reveals God's character—is He being worshiped as a King, Savior, Creator, Provider, or Deliverer?

Consider what response the verse calls for—does it invite joyful praise, deep reflection, surrender, or awe**?**

Step 4: Personalize and Apply the Verse to the Congregation

- ✓ Ask: How does this scripture apply today?
- ✓ Connect it with real-life experiences—is there a testimony, a challenge, or a recent event that makes this verse especially powerful?
- ✓ Use inclusive language like "we," "us," and "our" to help the congregation engage. Example: "This verse reminds us that no matter what we face, our God is worthy of our praise!"

Step 5: Structure the Exhortation Clearly

A well-structured exhortation keeps the congregation engaged. Use this simple format:

- ✓ Introduce the Scripture – Read it clearly and with conviction.
- ✓ Explain Its Meaning Briefly – Give one or two sentences summarizing the main message.

- ✓ Connect It to Worship – Show how this verse calls us to respond in worship.
- ✓ Encourage Engagement – Lead the people into action (lifting hands, singing with joy, bowing in reverence).

Step 6: Declare and Prophesy with Boldness

Speak with faith and authority, declaring the truth of God's Word.

Use declarations to stir faith—Example: "Church, let's lift our voices and praise our King because He is enthroned in our praises!"

Let the Holy Spirit lead—Be sensitive to His prompting, whether it's to go deeper, wait in silence, or shift the direction of worship.

Final Words

A worship leader is more than just a singer; you are a minister of God's presence. Your exhortations should not be just words but spiritual keys that unlock faith, shift atmospheres, and lead people into deeper encounters with the Lord. As you develop your exhortations using the Word of God, remember:

- ✓ Stay rooted in Scripture – God's Word carries power.
- ✓ Seek the Holy Spirit's guidance – He knows what the people need.
- ✓ Speak with passion and conviction – Your faith will ignite faith in others.
- ✓ Encourage participation – Worship is not a performance but a collective offering to God.

May this book serve as a tool to help you grow in your calling, and may every exhortation you give draw people closer to the heart of God.

Worship the Lord with all your heart, for He alone is worthy! **Amen.**

About the Author
'GERARD ASSEY'

Gerard Assey is a Graduate in Economics, a PGD in Management (HRD) and holds a Doctorate in Leadership. Gerard holds several International Qualifications in Sales, Debt Collection, Training & Teaching, and is a 'Fellow' of the prestigious 'Institute of Sales & Marketing Management'-UK, a Certified NLP Practitioner, a 'Certified Trainer', an 'Accredited Management Teacher-Behavioral Sciences', a 'Certified Competency Facilitator', a 'Certified Management Consultant'- (the International credentials of a professional management consultant, awarded in accordance with global standards of the ICMCI); and a Certification from the University of Michigan in 'Successful Negotiation: Essential Strategies and Skills'

He is also a Member of the 'National Association of Sales Professionals' backed with several years experience in varied industries, both in India and Overseas. He also holds an 'Etiquette Consultant' Certification from the USA (by Sue Fox, Author of Best Seller: 'Business Etiquette for Dummies'. She has trained some of the top celebrities' world over). He was also a recipient of a scholarship for extensive training in Japan on 'Corporate Management for India'.

Gerard Assey is 'Founder & Chief Corporate Trainer' of the Group: '**Citius, Altius, Fortius Unlimited**'- an organization that **celebrated 20 years of Glorious Service** in 2021, focusing on 3 Core Competencies:

People. Performance. Profit; in functional areas of Sales & Marketing, HR & Organizational Development, covering Recruitment, Training & Consultancy!

Having managed organizations with large Sales Forces in India & Overseas, his specialization cover extensive areas of Sales Training (All levels - Presentation, Negotiation, Key/ Strategic Accounts Management & Managerial Skills for all sectors), Bid Proposal/ Capture Planning/ Management Trainings, Retail Sales, Customer Service & Customer Retention Programs, Training for Prevention & Collection of Debt, Self & Personal Development Programs (Time Management, Teamwork & Team Building, Business Etiquette & Personal Grooming, Leadership & Managerial Skills, People Management Skills, Train-the-Trainer etc), including preparation of Custom-designed Business Manuals for Internal (HR, Induction, and Sales etc) & External use (Instruction, User Manuals).

Gerard has successfully conducted over 6450 Trainings & Workshops (as of Mar '25) all across India, Middle East, Africa, Europe & S.E. Asia. Besides public programs conducted regularly, both in India & Overseas, he has some of the top names as clients whom he services from Single Owners to large Public & Government undertakings, covering all sectors, for their in-house needs.

His website: www.CollectionSkills.com is the only one in this part of the world to be featured in the 'Collections & Credit Risk Magazine-USA' under 'Who's Who in Training' and ranks TOP, along with other websites listed below on most search engines.

Gerard is author of 180 books already (Mar 2025), all the books being available on all online platforms and outlets as E-books and Paperbacks

A few of our business related books:

1. Bite-sized Bits on Commonsense Management
2. Heart to Heart on Life's Principles'
3. How to become a Successful Manager
4. The Sales Professionals' Master Workbook of S.Y.S.T.E.M.S
5. The Professional Business Email Etiquette Handbook & Guide
6. The Professional Business Video-Conferencing Etiquette Handbook & Guide
7. Professional Presentation Skills
8. Exceptional Customer Service
9. Professional Tele-Marketing Skills
10. Professional Debt Collection Skills
11. The G.R.E.A.T. Sales & Service Workbook
12. Sales Training Advantage for Results (*The Ultimate Sales Training Manual to enable you stand out as a S.T.A.R.*)
13. CEO Daily Planner & Organizer
14. The Sales Professionals' Master Daily Planner
15. The Professional Debt Collector's Master Daily Planner
16. My Daily Planner & Organizer
17. MY EMERGENCY INFORMATION RECORD (Family Emergency & Peace of Mind Planner)
18. The Ultimate Therapist & Counselors Planner and Organizer
19. Building an Ethical Workplace
20. Managing Relationships at Work
21. Managing Business Meetings Effectively
22. Effective Delegation Skills
23. Goal Setting for Success
24. B2B Selling by Email
25. Professional Business Etiquette & Grooming
26. Dining Etiquette & Table Manners
27. Effective Networking Skills
28. Grooming, Etiquette & Manners for Teens, Young Adults & Future Leaders
29. Inter-Personal Skills
30. Get Ready, Get Hired!
31. Selling in a Recession

32. Effective Receivables Management in an Economic Downturn!
33. Real Estate & Property Sales Training
34. Credit Sales & Accounts Receivable Management
35. Selling Skills for Real Estate & Property Advisors
36. Take G.R.E.A.T. C.A.R.E!
37. Spa, Salon & Health Club Selling Skills
38. Selling Travel, Holiday & MICE Services
39. Selling Skills for Spa's, Salons & Health Clubs
40. Retailing in Salons & Spas
41. Selling Holiday, Vacation, Tours & Packages
42. The Power of Sales Referrals
43. Selling Luxury
44. Technical Selling Skills
45. Financial Advisors Sales Training
46. Dealing with Burnout at Work Monopolize Your Markets
47. Selling to Affluent Customers
48. Growing up with Grace
49. Financial Selling Skills
50. *The Effective Manager's Guide: Key Skills to Thrive*
51. From Aspiring to Inspiring: A Guide for New Managers on the Rise
52. The Power of Focus
53. Selling with Integrity: Sell Like Jesus The Perfect Role Model!
54. 31 Habits of Champions: Your 31-Day Journey to Greatness
55. Rejecting Grasshopper Talk: From Grasshopper to Giant-Killer-*Defeating Giants Daily!*
56. Navigate the AI-Powered Future of Bid & Proposals: Up-Skill to Stay Relevant with Alternative Career Paths & Opportunities
57. Hiring Sales Winners
58. Present with Impact
59. Success Unlocked: *Breaking Free from Habits that Hold You Back*
60. Complaints to Cheers, Feedback to Gold: Mastering Complaints Management
61. Thriving Together: *Cultivating Diversity, Equity, and Inclusion*
62. Coaching Skills for Sales Managers

63. Soaring to Success in Business & Leadership: Swifter, Higher, Stronger!
64. From Classroom to Podium: A Student's Guide to Powerful Public Speaking & Presentation Skills
65. Developing Self-Discipline
66. The CEO's 31-Day Power Plan: Unlocking Success through Essential Traits
67. Credibility Matters
68. A Winning Attitude
69. Bid & Proposal Management Using AI
70. Sales Forecasting: A Practical & Proven Guide to Strategic Sales Forecasting
71. Elevate & Energize: *50 Dynamic & Fun Activities for Peak Workplace Morale*
72. 'Sales SOS! Sales on Fire! *30 Days to Conquer Chaos & the Nightmares of Success!'*
73. Mastering Sales Managerial Skills: *Building High-Performing Teams & Driving Exceptional Results*
74. Eagle-Eyed Leadership: Unleashing the Power of 31 Lessons from Eagles
75. The Ultimate Employee Training Guide: *Training Today, Leading Tomorrow*
76. Being More Accountable at Work
77. Creating a Culture of Continuous Improvement
78. Effective Questioning & Listening Skills
79. The Power of Value Selling
80. The Growth Mindset
81. Mastering Professional Help Desk Skills
82. The Power to Lead with Empathy
83. Being Prepared: The Key to Unlocking Success
84. Youthful Spark-Youth Energizers, Activities and Games-Igniting the Fun in Youth
85. Ignite your Motivation for Success
86. Elevate Your Executive Presence: *Your Roadmap to Executive Excellence*
87. Smart Decisions: *Mastering Problem Solving with Strategic Solutions for Business Success*
88. Strategic Planning: *Developing and Implementing Strategic Plans to Achieve Long-Term Business Goals*
89. The Power of Stay Interviews
90. Developing G.R.I.T.
91. Adaptability

92. Diagnosis- *A Key Skill for Leadership*
93. The Burnout-Proof Salesperson: *The Master Guide to Preventing Stress & Burnout*- Strategies for Thriving in Sales
94. Learning from Failure: *Keys to Success*
95. Customer Success Management
96. Overcoming the Killers of Motivation
97. The C-Suite Code: *Mastering Skills for Executive Excellence'*
98. Dealing with Difficult Customers
99. Unlocking Your Potential: Mastering the Top 20 Life Skills for a Brighter Future
100. Nurturing Tomorrow's Leaders: *Essential Soft Skills Every Child Must Learn*
101. Lively & Fun Party Games for Seniors & Elders
102. Role Playing for Sales Champions: From Practice to Performance
103. Fun and Exciting Party Games for Kids
104. Case Studies for Sales
105. Role-Playing for Unbeatable Customer Service
106. Case Studies in Customer Service
107. Case Studies in Winning Negotiations
108. Case Studies in Management & Leadership
109. Case Studies in Human Resources & Talent Management
110. CEO Success Blueprint: The Essential Toolkit for CEOs and C-Level Executives
111. The Salesperson's Self-Coaching Guide: *Master Your Own Self-Coaching Plan for Success*
112. Overcoming Procrastination: *Your Ultimate Guide to Stop Delaying and Start Living Your Best Life*
113. When True Colors Are Exposed: *The Journey to Unmasking Humanity*
114. Life-Changing Habits for Teens: Teen Success Blueprint for a Bright Future
115. Workplace Stress-Free: *Proven Strategies to Thrive at Work and Beyond*
116. Objection Overruled: *The Ultimate Guide to Turning 'No' into 'Yes'*

From the Ministry side, Gerard graduated in the very first batch of Charis Bible College-India & had for over 9 years served as a Part-time Faculty at Charis Bible College-Chennai (Andrew Wommack Ministries-Colorado, USA).
He is also a graduate of the Advanced Mentorship Program (AMP) and the Circle Of Ministerial Engagement (C.O.M.E.) of Prophet Jerome Fernando and a Spiritual Son of the Esteemed Prophet.
An accomplished author of several Secular & Christian Books, Gerard has been on the board of a few international organizations and boasts of being the SON of the MOST HIGH GOD: An ordinary guy following an extraordinary GOD!

...And some of his most recent Christian Books being:

1. A Bouquet of Praises for My KING
2. Christian Jokes for the Serious Religious' Folks!
3. Jesus Healed You!
4. Praise24Ever! (also in Tamil version)
5. The 5G Network of GOD
6. Building Faith over F.E.A.R- FACE EVERYTHING AND RISE with JESUS
7. Hebrew and Greek Praise and Worship Words
8. Godly Mothers' and Grandmothers' Bible Story time for Kids!
9. Miracles of Jesus in Pictures
10. Raise your Praise all 365 Days
11. Thanking GOD with an Attitude of Gratitude
12. Meditating on the Attributes of GOD
13. Puppet Scripts
14. Alcohol Ruins, JESUS Reforms, Renews & Restores!
15. Habakkuk 2:2 Christian Daily Journal, Planner & Organizer
16. ABC of GOD's Word for Handwriting Practice
17. Daily Bible Verse Handwriting Practice (Building Godly Character & Faith through Cursive Handwriting Practice!)
18. Guiding Light: Fun & Faith-Building Bible Activities for Children
19. Rejecting Grasshopper Talk: From Grasshopper to Giant-Killer-*Defeating Giants Daily!*
20. Teen Titans of Faith: *Building Courage, Determination & Christ-like-Esteem*
21. I AM Empowered: *Unleashing Divine Power with Positive Declarations*
22. Be A Solution Provider-*From Passion to Purpose*: *A Biblical Guide to Being the Answer to the World!*
23. Miracles of JESUS

24. Parables of Jesus for a Meaningful Life!
25. A Grateful Heart: Importance of Sharing Testimonies of GOD's Grace
26. Melodies of Worship to JESUS: 31 Songs of Praise & Worship From My Heart to HIS!
27. I AM SO BLESSED!
28. My Daily Cup of Energizer
29. 31 Leadership Lessons *from* Jesus- *The Supreme Leader*
30. Peace Amidst Storms: A Biblical Guide to Conquering S.T.R.E.S.S.
31. Rise Above: 20 Biblical Eagle Lessons for Life's Triumphs
32. Godly Goal Setting: *The FAITHFUL Blueprint for a Purpose-Driven Life*
33. The Profound Attributes of our Mighty GOD: Understanding the 10S's of the Almighty
34. Worship Now, Worship Forever: *A Journey from Earthly Praise to Eternal Glory*
35. Unceasing Praise & Worship: *365 Days to Worship the King*
36. The ROAR Within: *Living with Purpose and Authority through the Power of the Holy Spirit*
37. From Potential to Purpose: Unlocking and Multiplying Your Talents & Gifts for Kingdom Impact
38. Songs from the Heart: *Worshipping GOD in Your Own Tune & Melody*
39. Awakening Praise & Worship: Hebrew & Greek Words to Raise Your Praise
40. Sing a NEW Song to the LORD Everyday: *Daily Devotions of Praise & Worship to Lift Your Heart & Glorify HIS Name*
41. *The* A.R.O.M.A. of True Worship: *Creating Worship That Delights God*
42. Becoming A Kingdom Champion: *Embracing God's Call for a Life of Purpose & Victory*
43. The Busy Businessman's Daily Devotional: 366 Crisp Truths to Start Your Day Strong
44. The Teacher's Heart: *Daily Devotions for Educators*
45. Anchored! *A 31-Day Devotional for Students Facing Life's Challenges*
46. Suddenly! Unlocking Unorthodox Breakthroughs through Unusual Worship
47. Overcoming Adversity: *Lessons from the Bible for Modern Challenges*
48. LORD, Don't do it without me
49. Kingdom Leadership: *Biblical Principles for Modern Leaders*
50. Heartprints of God- *Growing God's Way:* Daily Devotions for Kids

to Shine Bright

51. Send Judah First: Let your Praises Go up First to See the Mighty Move of GOD
52. DIVINE MOMENTS: *Recognizing, Embracing, Preparing, and Walking into Life-Changing Encounters with God*
53. Be a Builder in the Kingdom: *The C.E.M.E.N.T. Guide to Creating a Lasting Legacy*
54. Unshakable: *Pillars of Godly Womanhood* (Pillars of Faith That Changed History)
55. Lead Like a Shepherd: *14 Essential Traits for Pastoral Excellence*
56. The Worship Leader's Arsenal: *Powerful Exhortations to Ignite Thanksgiving, Praise & Worship*

Besides regularly contributing to business & trade journals, including international ones such as the 'Creative Training Techniques' and the 'Sales News' of the U.S.A, He is also a member of several prestigious bodies & trade associations, having participated in many Conferences & Workshops in India & Overseas.

Prior to his last assignment of leading & managing a large MNC as head, Gerard had a 3-year stint in the Middle East as a Consultant with a leading British Consultancy Firm.

As the past 'Official Country Representative' for the International Business Award- 'THE STEVIES'-(the business world's own Oscar) for about 4 years- he ensured a few Indian companies that qualify for the same every year!

Gerard can be contacted at:
Email: training@Sales-Training.in,training@CollectionSkills.com
Websites:

www.Sales-Training.in
www.EtiquetteWorks.in
www.CollectionSkills.com
www.RetailSalesTraining.in
www.SalesTrainingIndia.com
www.ManualPreparation.com
www.TrainingWithPuppets.com
www.FirstContactAcademy.com
www.SalesAndMarketingRecruiter.com

Our TRAININGS that can help your team

- ✓ **Sales Effectiveness**: Selling Skills for any Sector: Service/ Logistics/ FMCG Realty/ Insurance & Finance/ Media/ SPA's, Health Clubs & Salons/ Key Account Management, Effective Negotiation Skills/ Bid & Proposal Management Skills/ Retail Sales Training: Any Sector (Auto, Jewelry, Clothing, Luxury etc)
- ✓ **Customer Service Skills**-Complaints Handling & Customer Retention
- ✓ **Debt Prevention & Collection Skills**
- ✓ **Etiquette & Grooming**
- ✓ **Leadership & Managerial Skills**
- ✓ **Self & Personal Development Skills**: Presentation Skills/ Effective Communication Skills/Business Proposal Writing Skills/ Problem Solving & Decision Making Skills/ Empowering Secretaries-The perfect PA! (For Secretaries & PA's)/ Effective Time Management/ Teamwork & Teambuilding/ P.R.I.D.E- **P**ersonal **R**esponsibility **I**n **D**elivering **E**xcellence

www.ingramcontent.com/pod-product-compliance
Ingram Content Group UK Ltd.
Pitfield, Milton Keynes, MK11 3LW, UK
UKHW021341190726
13845UKWH00027B/669

9 788198 569196